NOTE TO PARENTS

This well known fairytale has been specially written and adapted for 'first readers', that is, for children who are just beginning to read by themselves. However, for those not yet able to read, then why not read this story aloud to your child, pointing to the words and talking about the pictures? There is a word list at the back of the book which identifies difficult words and explains their meaning in the context of the story.

The Emperor's New Clothes

retold by Pat Posner
illustrated by Gill Guile

Copyright © MCMLXXXVIII by World International Publishing Limited.
All rights reserved.
Published in Great Britain by World International Publishing Limited.
An Egmont Company, Egmont House,
P.O. Box 111, Great Ducie Street,
Manchester M60 3BL.
Printed in Italy.
ISBN 7235 8885 6

Once there was an Emperor
who loved new clothes.
He loved them even better
than he loved people.

He wore something new every hour.
Sometimes he changed his clothes
ten times a day!

The Emperor heard
about a grand parade in the town.
I must lead the parade, he thought.
I will wear the best clothes
anyone has ever seen.

"I will give gold to the tailor
who makes me the finest material
in the land," said the Emperor.

Every tailor took beautiful material
to show the Emperor.

But he could not decide
which was the finest!
This made him feel sad.

A whole week went past.
The Emperor still had not seen
any material he liked.
Then two strange tailors
came to him.

"We can make the best clothes
you have ever seen,"
they told the Emperor.
"And we will make them magic!
Only wise men will see the clothes.
Fools will see nothing at all!"

"So if my helpers do not see
the clothes, then they are fools,"
said the Emperor.
"I only want
wise men working for me!"

He told the two tailors
to start work at once.
A servant took them to a room
where they could make
the Emperor his new clothes.

When they were alone
the tailors laughed and laughed.
"Everyone will pretend to see
the clothes," they said. "Nobody
will want to look like a fool!"

Next day, the tailors
worked busily away.
But their spinning wheel was empty.
Yet everybody pretended to see
the most beautiful silk
in the whole world!

Even the Emperor
could not see any silk.
But he did not want
to be called a fool.
"What beautiful silk," he said.

Then the tailors pretended
to weave the silk.
Every day the Emperor's helpers
went to see them.
And every day they told the Emperor
that his new clothes were beautiful.

The Emperor was very happy.
He gave the tailors lots of gold.
The naughty tailors were getting
very rich.

The day of the grand parade arrived.
In the Emperor's dressing room
the tailors pretended to dress him
in his new clothes.

Of course, the Emperor
could not really see any fine clothes.
He could only see his underwear!
But he did not want to seem a fool.
"These are the best clothes
I have ever worn," he said.

His helpers said he looked splendid.
The naughty tailors turned
and giggled to themselves.

He did look funny
when he sat on his horse.
But everybody pretended
they could see the finest clothes
in the land.

While the Emperor led the parade,
the tailors took all the gold.
Then they ran from the town
and were never seen again.

Many people saw the parade.
They all wanted to see
the Emperor's new clothes.
He waved as he rode past.
Oh, he did look funny
in only his underwear!

Of course, the people
could not see any fine, new clothes.
But they all pretended they could.
They did not want to look like fools.

Suddenly, a little boy shouted,
"The Emperor is only wearing
his underwear!"
The Emperor knew it was true.

"The two tailors tricked me," he said.
"They have taken all my gold.
Now I know that people
are more important than clothes.
From today, my people
will always come first."
And the Emperor kept his promise.

New words

Did you see a lot of new words in the story? Here is a list of some hard words from the story, and what they mean.

arrived
when the day of the parade came

beautiful
this means 'very lovely'

decide
when the Emperor
could not make up his mind

Emperor
an emperor is a like a king

important
something that is special

material
it is another word for cloth

naughty
the tailors were bad